ENGLISH - TURKISH

STAR CHILDREN'S PICTURE DICTIONARY

Editor
Babita Varma

STAR CHILDREN'S PICTURE DICTIONARY

Varma, Babita (Editor)

Published by :

STAR PUBLICATIONS PVT. LTD.
Asaf Ali Road, New Delhi-110002 (INDIA)
email : starpub@satyam.net.in

Revised Edition : 2006

ISBN : 81-7650-206-5

THIS DICTIONARY
has been published in Arabic, Bengali, Chinese, Croation, Danish, Farsi, Gujarati,
Hindi, Vietnamese, Malayalam, Norwegian, Punjabi, Portuguese, Somali, Spanish,
Tamil, Turkish and Urdu. Other languages are in press.

**To
Children of all ages;
whatever language
they speak.**

FROM THE PUBLISHERS :

This unique colourful dictionary was first published in 1993, and was brought out in sololingual, bilingual and trilingual editions. Within a span of three years we could publish it in about 32 major languages of the world, and the Dictionary was acclaimed as one of the best pictorial dictionaries to teach various languages-not only to young children but also to those foreigners who wish to learn another language. It was acknowledged as a source to build wordpower and stimulate learning, specially among children.

However, on the basis of various suggestions received since its publication, the Editor decided to revise the whole dictionary by adding many new words and illustrations, as also changing the style. We are now pleased to present this dictionary with a new format. This dictionary now consists of over 1,000 words and colourful illustrations, which have been catagorised in 12 popular subjects. In case of bilingual editions, each word has been translated into the other language, and transliterated where necessary.

We are confident that readers will find this dictionary as a very useful presentation which will encourage browsing, and make learning fun for the young and old alike. Since this dictionary has been published in several languages of the world, it will be found as a timely contribution to multilingualism and multiculturalism.

INDEX

TURKISH ALPHABET

A a	B b	C c	Ç ç
D d	E e	F f	G g
Ğ ğ	H h	I ı	İ i
J j	K k	L l	M m
N n	O o	Ö ö	P p
R r	S s	Ş ş	T t
U u	Ü ü	V v	Y y
Z z			

A a B b C c D d

E e F f G g H h

I i J j K k L l

M m N n O o P p

Q q R r S s T t

U u V v W w X x

Y y Z z

NUMBERS

0		*zero*-**sıfır**
1		*one*-**bir**
2		*two*-**iki**
3		*three*-**üç**
4		*four*-**dört**
5		*five*-**beş**
6		*six*-**altı**
7		*seven*-**yedi**
8		*eight*-**sekiz**
9		*nine*-**dokuz**
10		*ten*-**on**

ANIMALS, BIRDS AND OTHER LIVING CREATURES

HAYVANLAR, KUŞLAR VE DİĞER CANLILAR

ant **karınca**	*bee* **arı**
ape **maymun**	*bird* **kuş**
bat **yarasa**	*bison* **bizon**
bear **ayı**	*buffalo* **manda**
beetle **kınkanatlı**	*bull* **boğa**

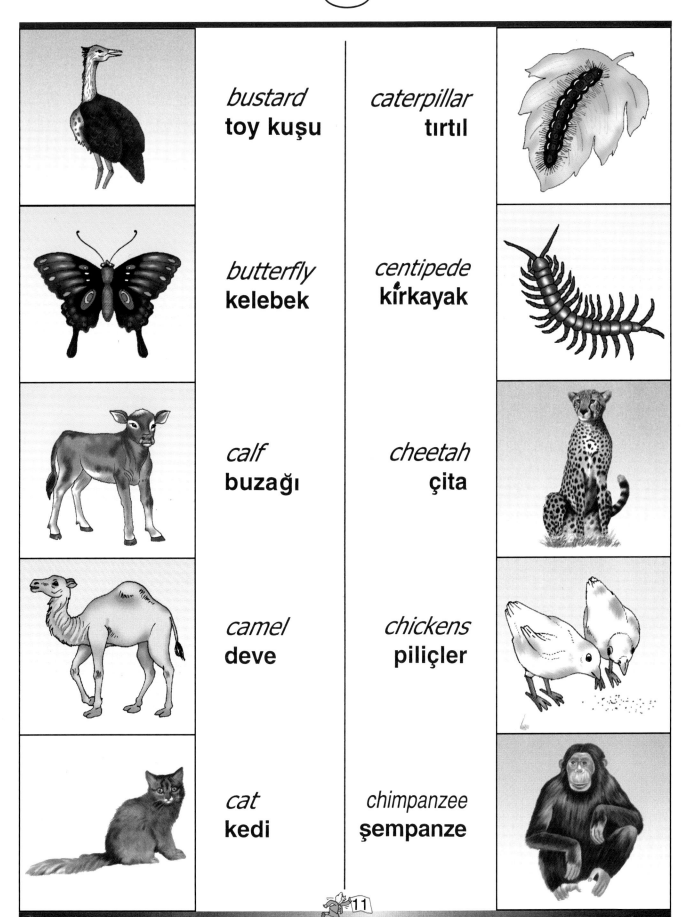

bustard **toy kuşu**	*caterpillar* **tırtıl**
butterfly **kelebek**	*centipede* **kırkayak**
calf **buzağı**	*cheetah* **çita**
camel **deve**	*chickens* **piliçler**
cat **kedi**	*chimpanzee* **şempanze**

cobra **kobra**	*crocodile* **timsah**
cock **horoz**	*crow* **karga**
cockroach hamamböceği	*cuckoo* **guguk kuşu**
cow **inek**	*deer* **geyik**
crab **yengeç**	*dinosaur* **dinozor**

dog **köpek**	*eel* **yılanbalığı**
dolphin **yunus balığı**	*earthworm* **solucan**
donkey **eşek**	*elephant* **fil**
duck **ördek**	*fish* **balık**
eagle **kartal**	*flamingos* **flaman kuşları**

fly	goat
sinek	**keçi**

fox	goose
tilki	**kaz**

frog	grass-hopper
kurbağa	**çayır çekirgesi**

giraffe	hare
zürafa	**tavşan**

	hen
	tavuk

heron **balıkçıl**	*jackal* **çakal**
hippo - potamus **su aygırı**	*kangaroo* **kanguru**
honey- bee **balarısı**	*kiwi* **kivi**
horse **at**	*ladybird* **uğur böceği**
insects **böcekler**	*leopard* **leopar**

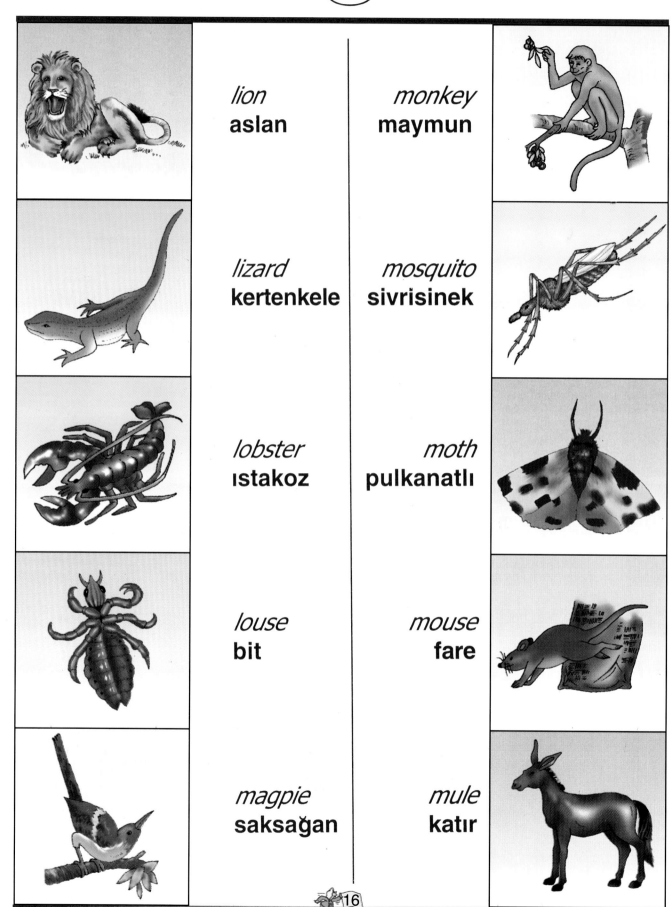

lion **aslan**	*monkey* **maymun**
lizard **kertenkele**	*mosquito* **sivrisinek**
lobster **ıstakoz**	*moth* **pulkanatlı**
louse **bit**	*mouse* **fare**
magpie **saksağan**	*mule* **katır**

myna **mina**	*ox* **öküz**
octopus **ahtapot**	*platypus* **platipus**
ostrich **deve kuşu**	*panda* **panda**
otter **su samuru**	*panther* **panter**
owl **baykuş**	*parrot* **papağan**

peacock **tavuk kuşu**	*polar bear* **kutup ayısı**
pelican **kaşıkcı kuşu**	*porcupine* **oklu kirpi**
penguin **penguen**	*prawn* **karides**
puppy **köpek yavrusu**	*quail* **bıldırcın**
pigeon **güvercin**	*rabbit* **ada tavşanı**

rat **sıçan**	*sheep* **koyun**
rhinoceros **gergedan**	*snake* **yılan**
scorpion **akrep**	*sparrow* **serçe**
seal **fok**	*spider* **örümcek**
shark **köpek balığı**	*squirrel* **sincap**

stork **leylek**	*vulture* **akbaba**
swan **kuğu**	*woodpecker* **ağaçkakan**
tiger **kaplan**	*wolf* **kurt**
tortoise kara kaplumbağası	*yak* Tibet sığırı
turtle su kaplumbağası	*zebra* **zebra**

FOOD, DRINKS AND OTHER THINGS TO EAT

YİYECEKLER VE İÇECEKLER

almonds **bademler**	*biscuits* **bisküvi**
apple **elma**	*bread* **ekmek**
apricot **kayısı**	*brinjal* **patlıcan**
bananas **muzlar**	*butter* **tereyağı**
beetroot **pancar**	*cabbage* **lahana**

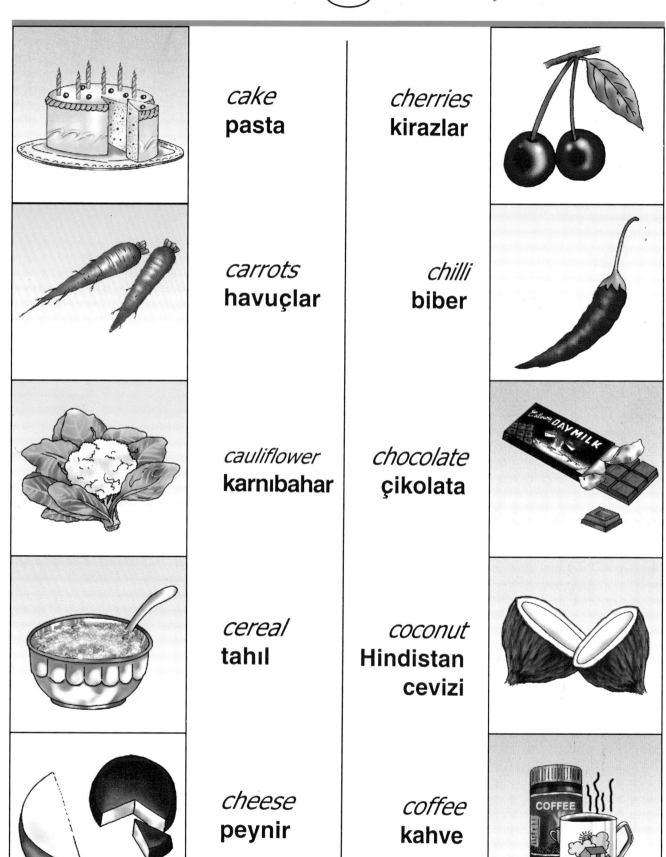

cake **pasta**	*cherries* **kirazlar**
carrots **havuçlar**	*chilli* **biber**
cauliflower **karnıbahar**	*chocolate* **çikolata**
cereal **tahıl**	*coconut* **Hindistan cevizi**
cheese **peynir**	*coffee* **kahve**

cucumber **salatalık**	*fig* **incir**
currants **kuşüzümü**	*fruit* **meyveler**
dates **hurma**	*garlic* **sarmısak**
durian **durian**	*ginger* **zencefil**
egg **yumurta**	*grapes* **üzüm**

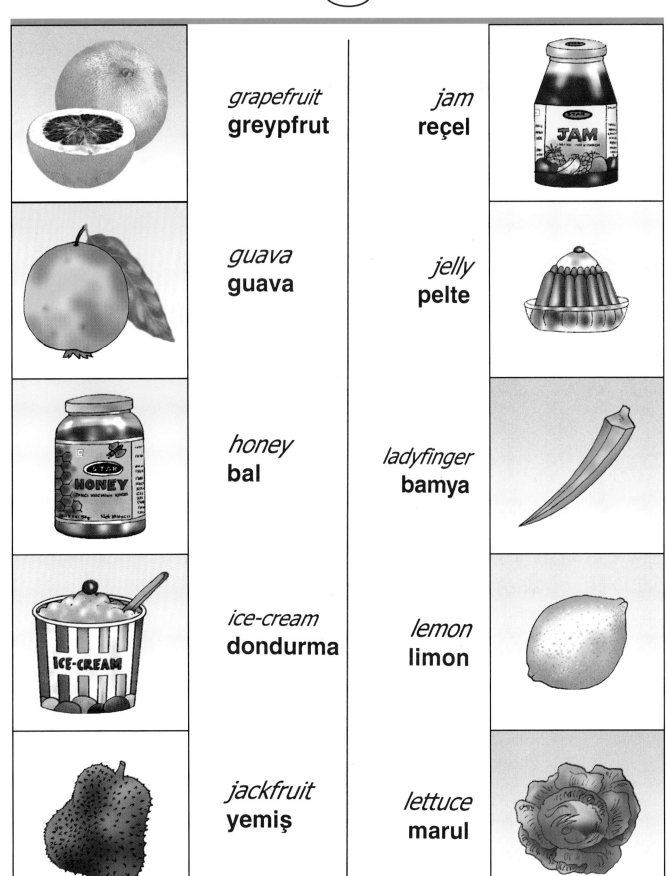

grapefruit **greypfrut**	*jam* **reçel**
guava **guava**	*jelly* **pelte**
honey **bal**	*ladyfinger* **bamya**
ice-cream **dondurma**	*lemon* **limon**
jackfruit **yemiş**	*lettuce* **marul**

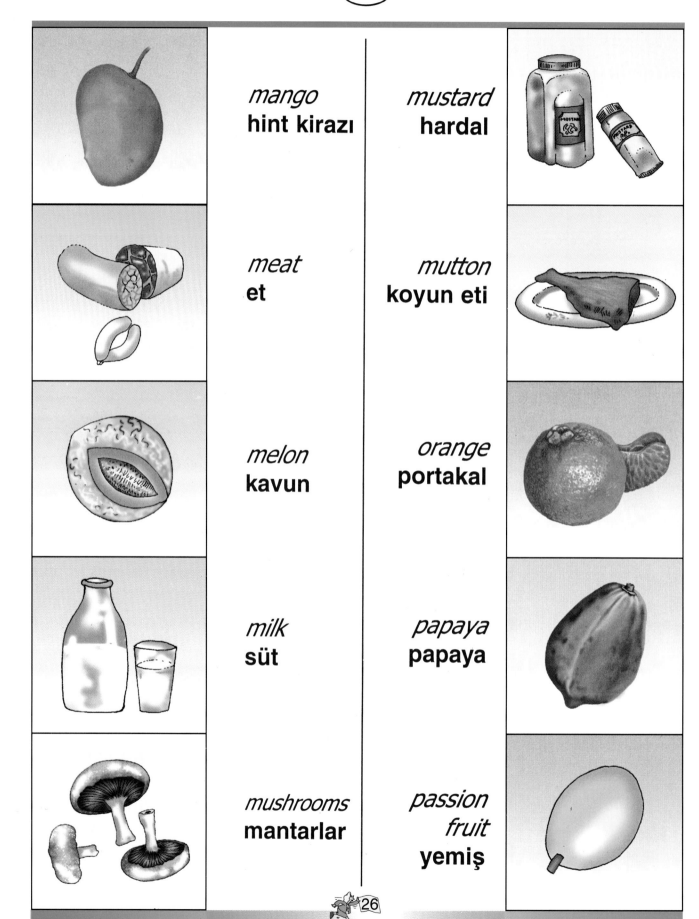

	mango **hint kirazı**	*mustard* **hardal**	
	meat **et**	*mutton* **koyun eti**	
	melon **kavun**	*orange* **portakal**	
	milk **süt**	*papaya* **papaya**	
	mushrooms **mantarlar**	*passion fruit* **yemiş**	

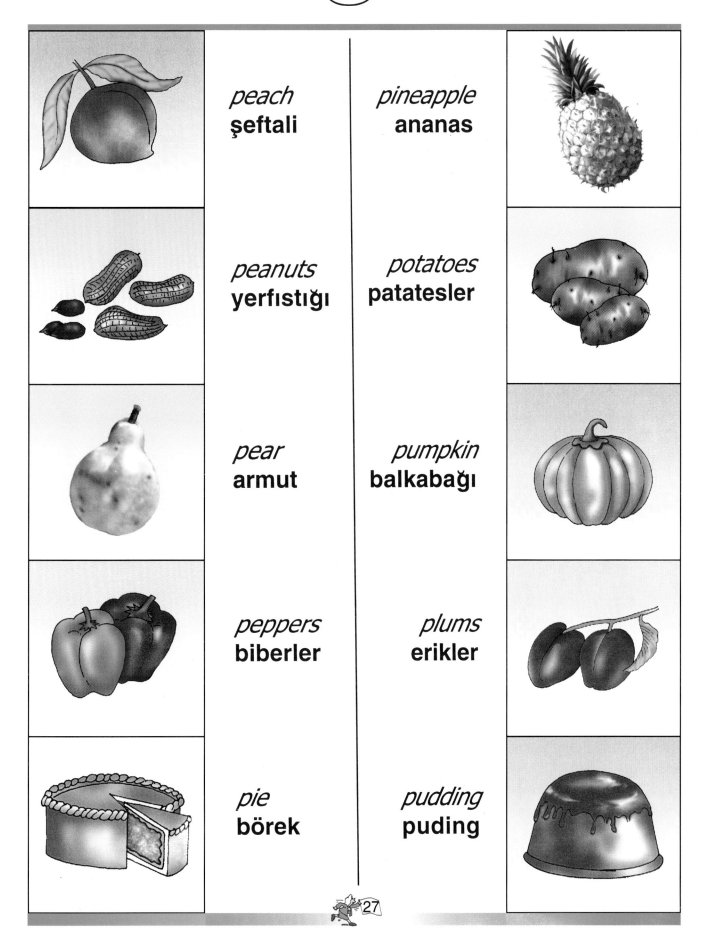

peach **şeftali**	*pineapple* **ananas**
peanuts **yerfıstığı**	*potatoes* **patatesler**
pear **armut**	*pumpkin* **balkabağı**
peppers **biberler**	*plums* **erikler**
pie **börek**	*pudding* **puding**

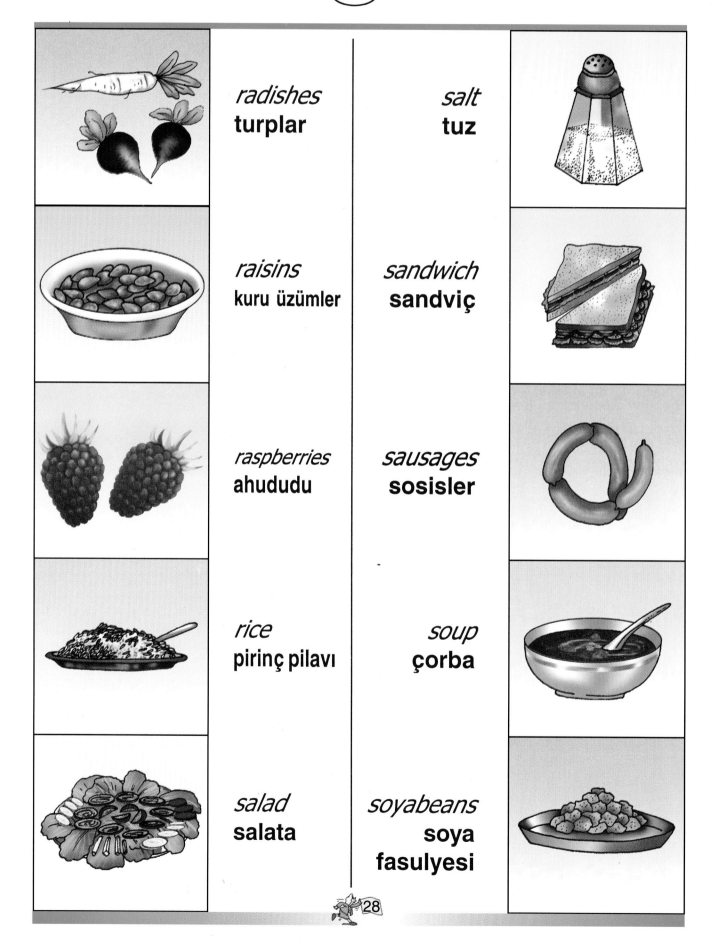

radishes
turplar

salt
tuz

raisins
kuru üzümler

sandwich
sandviç

raspberries
ahududu

sausages
sosisler

rice
pirinç pilavı

soup
çorba

salad
salata

soyabeans
**soya
fasulyesi**

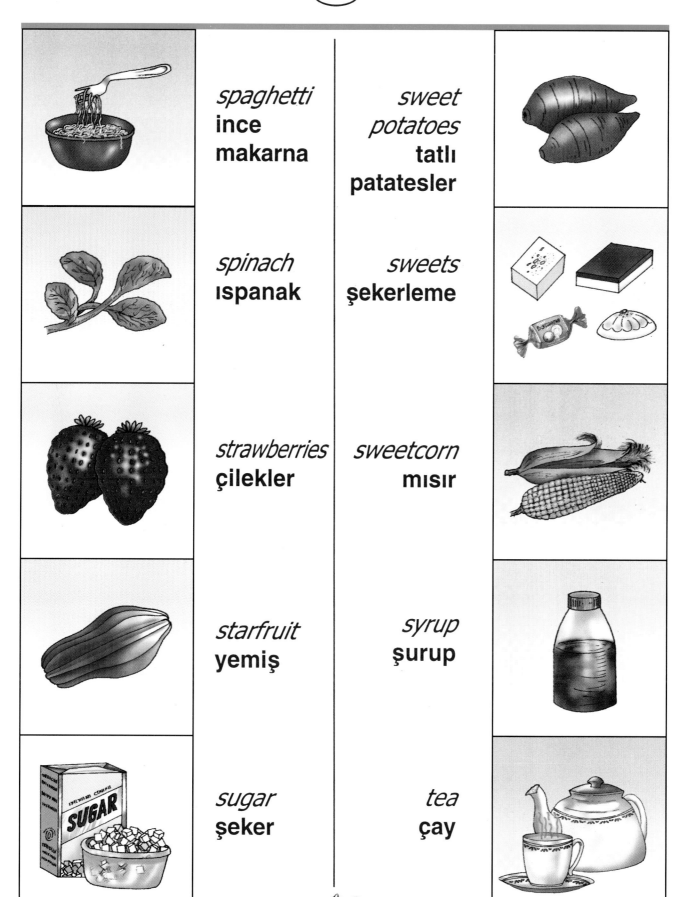

spaghetti **ince** **makarna**	*sweet* *potatoes* **tatlı** **patatesler**
spinach **ıspanak**	*sweets* **şekerleme**
strawberries **çilekler**	*sweetcorn* **mısır**
starfruit **yemiş**	*syrup* **şurup**
sugar **şeker**	*tea* **çay**

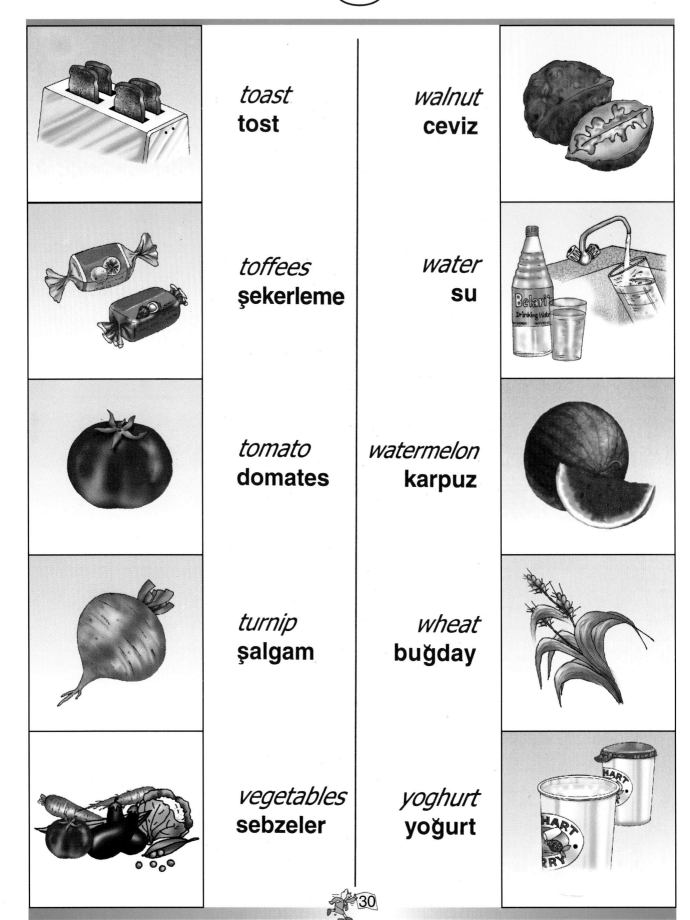

toast **tost**	*walnut* **ceviz**
toffees **şekerleme**	*water* **su**
tomato **domates**	*watermelon* **karpuz**
turnip **şalgam**	*wheat* **buğday**
vegetables **sebzeler**	*yoghurt* **yoğurt**

HOME

EV

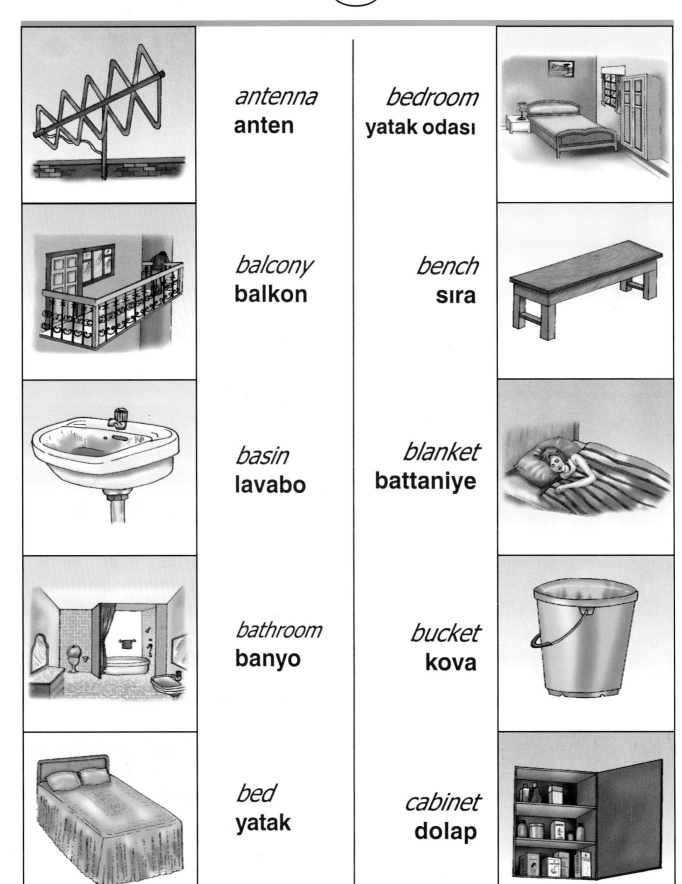

antenna **anten**	*bedroom* **yatak odası**
balcony **balkon**	*bench* **sıra**
basin **lavabo**	*blanket* **battaniye**
bathroom **banyo**	*bucket* **kova**
bed **yatak**	*cabinet* **dolap**

carpet
halı

cloth
kumaş

ceiling
tavan

cot
çocuk yatağı

chair
sandalye

cupboard
dolap

chandelier
avize

curtains
perdeler

chimneys
bacalar

door
kapı

drain **lağım**		*flower vase* **vazo**	
elevator **asansör**		*foam* **sünger**	
escalator **yürüyen merdiven**		*fork* **çatal**	
fences **tahta perdeler**		*garden* **bahçe**	
flats **apartman daireleri**		*garage* **garaj**	

gate
bahçe kapısı

home
ev

hose
hortum

kitchen
mutfak

letter-box
posta kutusu

mattress
somya

matchbox
kibrit kutusu

mop
paspas

necktie
kravat

oven
fırın

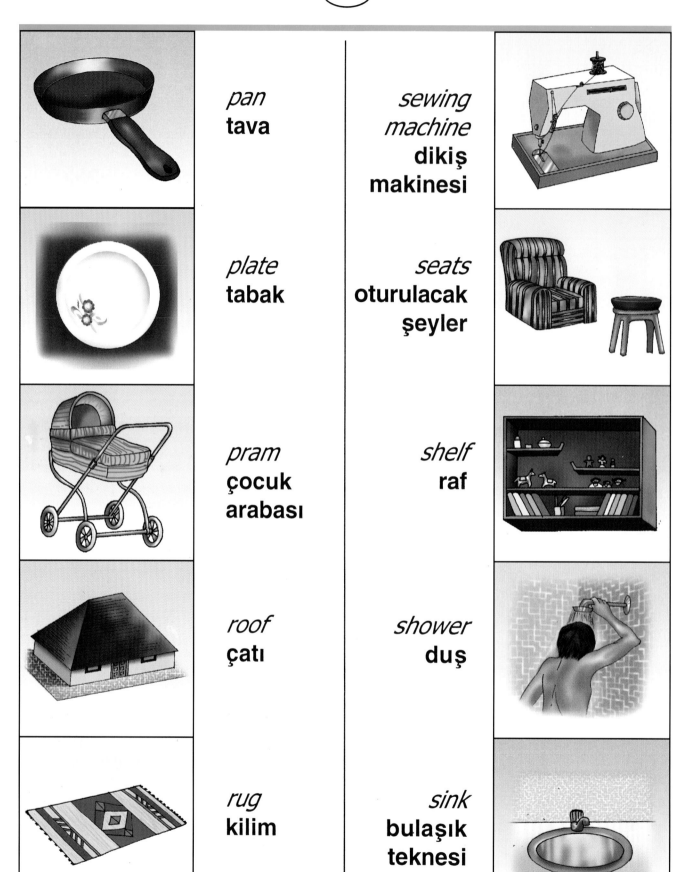

pan **tava**		*sewing machine* **dikiş makinesi**	
plate **tabak**		*seats* **oturulacak şeyler**	
pram **çocuk arabası**		*shelf* **raf**	
roof **çatı**		*shower* **duş**	
rug **kilim**		*sink* **bulaşık teknesi**	

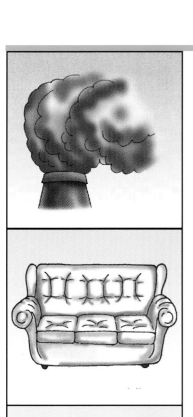

smoke
duman

toothbrush
diş fırçası

sofa
koltuk

tub
küvet

spanner
somun anahtarı

wall
duvar

stairs/ steps
merdiven

wardrobe
gardırop

toilet
tuvalet

window
pencere

bag **çanta**	*clock* **duvar saati**
glass **bardak**	*cushions* **minderler**
knife **bıçak**	*radio* **radyo**
refrigerator **buzdolabı**	*telephone* **telefon**
stove **ocak**	*table* **masa**

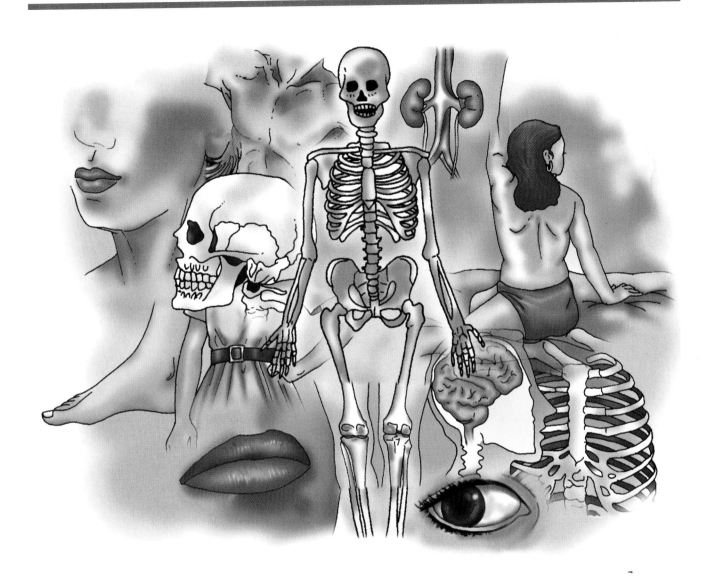

HUMAN BODY
İNSAN VÜCUDU

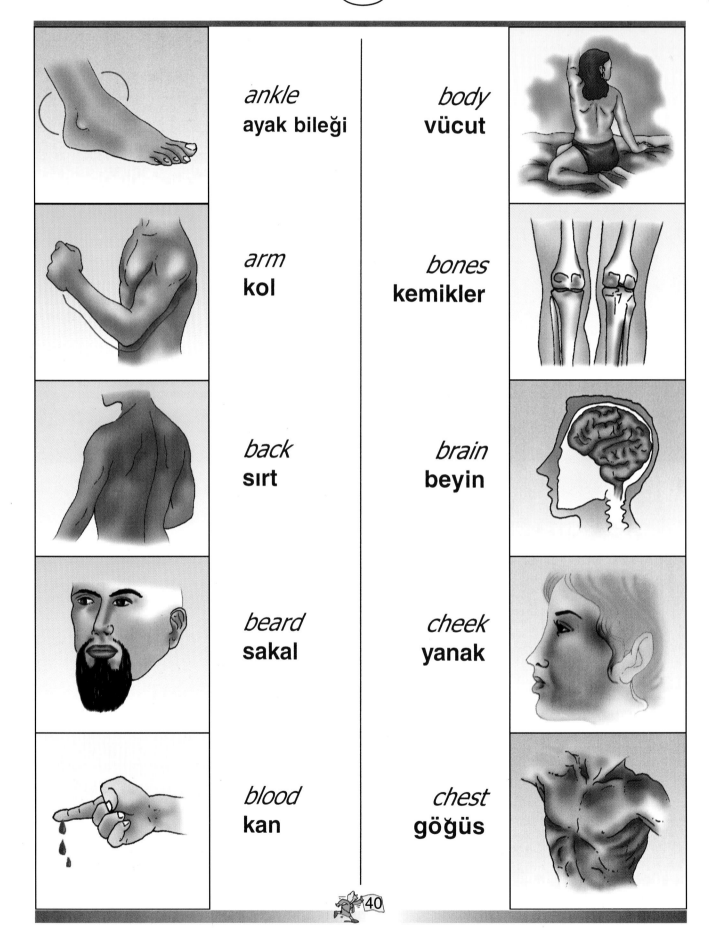

ankle **ayak bileği**	*body* **vücut**
arm **kol**	*bones* **kemikler**
back **sırt**	*brain* **beyin**
beard **sakal**	*cheek* **yanak**
blood **kan**	*chest* **göğüs**

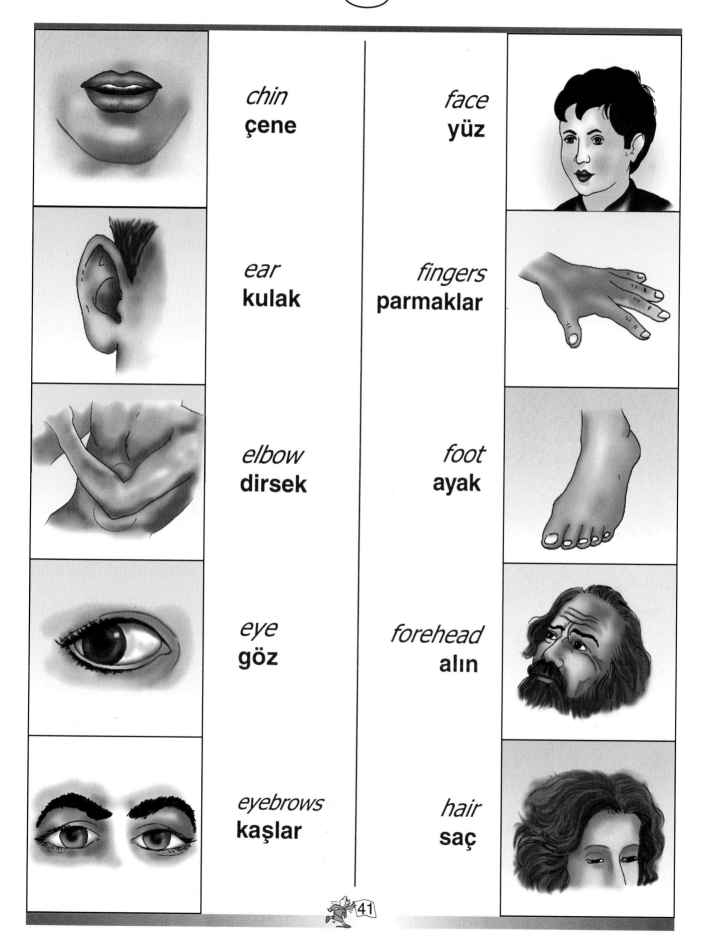

chin **çene**	*face* **yüz**
ear **kulak**	*fingers* **parmaklar**
elbow **dirsek**	*foot* **ayak**
eye **göz**	*forehead* **alın**
eyebrows **kaşlar**	*hair* **saç**

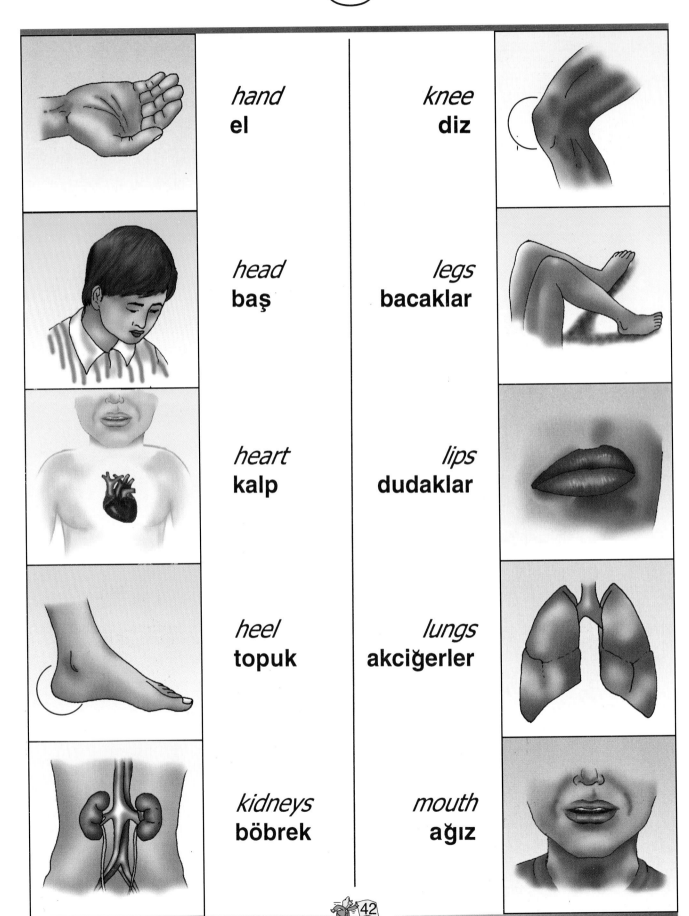

hand **el**	*knee* **diz**
head **baş**	*legs* **bacaklar**
heart **kalp**	*lips* **dudaklar**
heel **topuk**	*lungs* **akciğerler**
kidneys **böbrek**	*mouth* **ağız**

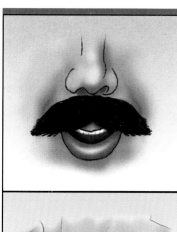

moustache
bıyık

palm
avuç

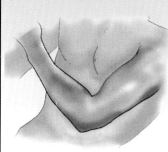

muscle
adele

ribs
kaburgalar

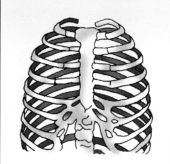

nails
tırnaklar

shoulders
omuzlar

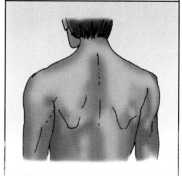

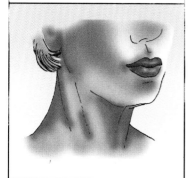

neck
boyun

skeleton
iskelet

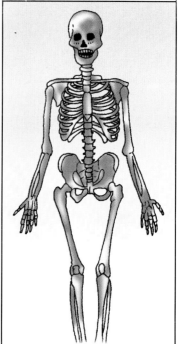

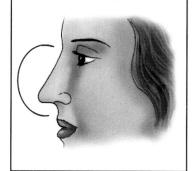

nose
burun

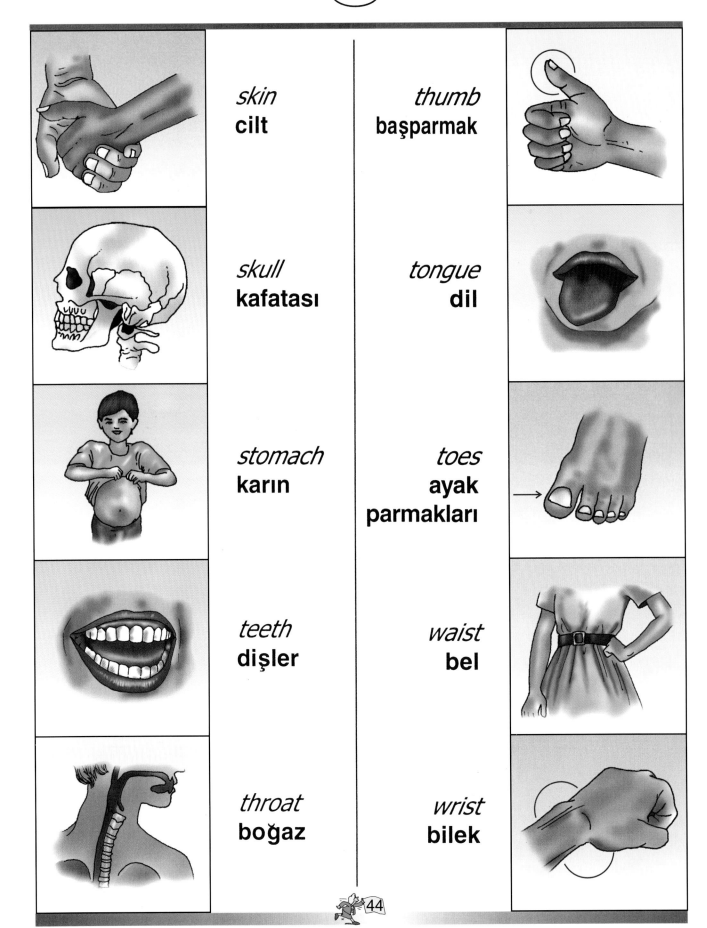

skin **cilt**	*thumb* **başparmak**
skull **kafatası**	*tongue* **dil**
stomach **karın**	*toes* **ayak parmakları**
teeth **dişler**	*waist* **bel**
throat **boğaz**	*wrist* **bilek**

MEASUREMENTS, SHAPES, COLOURS AND TIME

ÖLÇÜLER, ŞEKİLLER, RENKLER VE ZAMAN

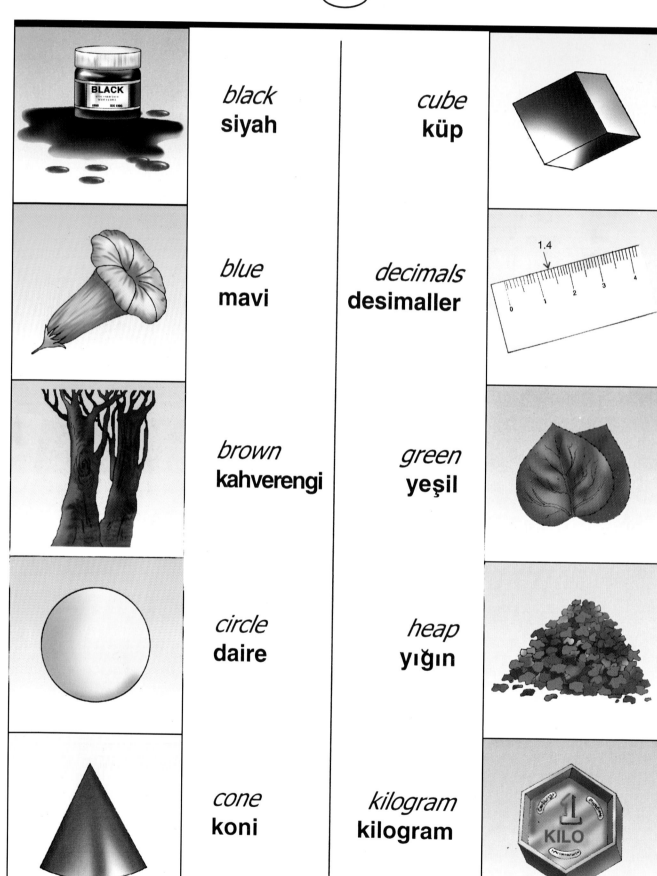

black **siyah**	*cube* **küp**
blue **mavi**	*decimals* **desimaller**
brown **kahverengi**	*green* **yeşil**
circle **daire**	*heap* **yığın**
cone **koni**	*kilogram* **kilogram**

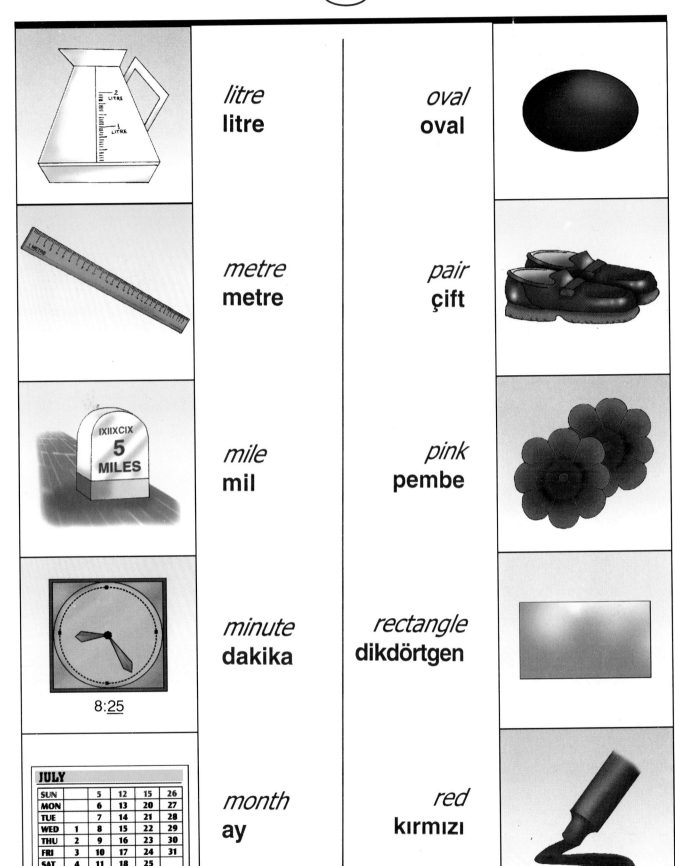

litre **litre**	*oval* **oval**
metre **metre**	*pair* **çift**
mile **mil**	*pink* **pembe**
minute **dakika**	*rectangle* **dikdörtgen**
month **ay**	*red* **kırmızı**

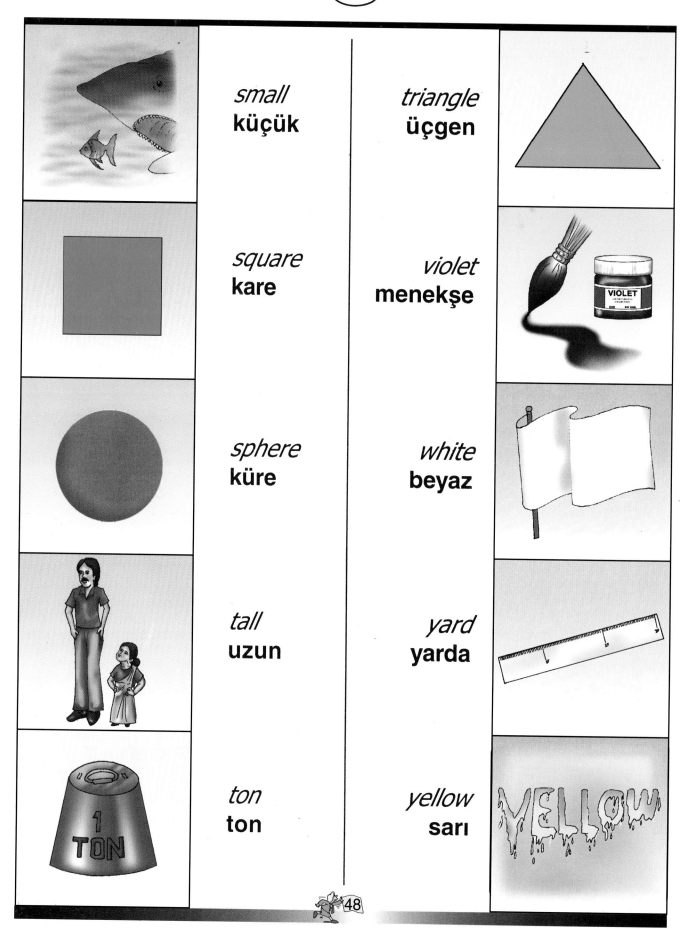

small **küçük**	*triangle* **üçgen**
square **kare**	*violet* **menekşe**
sphere **küre**	*white* **beyaz**
tall **uzun**	*yard* **yarda**
ton **ton**	*yellow* **sarı**

PEOPLE, COSTUMES AND ORNAMENTS

İNSANLAR, GİYSİLER VE SÜS EŞYALARI

actor **erkek oyuncu**	*astronaut* **astronot**
actress **kadın oyuncu**	*athlete* **atlet**
angel **melek**	*author* **yazar**
architect **mimar**	*baby* **bebek**
artist **sanatçı**	*baker* **fırıncı**

bandit **haydut**	*bride* **gelin**
bishop **piskopos**	*bridegroom* **damat**
blacksmith **demirci**	*captain* **kaptan**
blouse **bluz**	*caps* **kasketler**
boy **erkek çocuk**	*carpenter* **marangoz**

child
çocuk

daughter
kız evlat

clown
palyaço

dentist
diş doktoru

conductor
kondüktör

doctor
doktor

cook/chef
aşçı

driver
sürücü

dancers
dansçılar

dwarfs
cüceler

electrician **elektrikçi**	*king* **kral**
farmer **çiftçi**	*knight* **şövalye**
fire-fighter **itfaiyeci**	*lady* **bayan**
girl **kız**	*man* **adam**
jacket **ceket**	*mechanic* **makineci**

miner **madenci**	*nun* rahibe
merchant **tüccar**	*nurse* **hemşire**
monk **keşiş**	*painter* **boyacı**
musicians **müzisyenler**	*pilot* **pilot**
necktie **kravat**	*plumber* **tesisatcı**

police officer
polis memuru

queen
kraliçe

porter
taşıyıcı

robber
soyguncu

postman
postacı

sailor
denizci

priest
rahip

shorts
şort

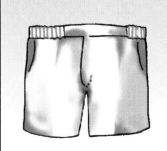

prince
prens

shopkeeper
dükkan sahibi

sisters
kızkardeşler

turban
sarık

soldier
asker

waiter
garson

solicitor
avukat

wife
eş

teacher
öğretmen

woman
kadın

thief
hırsız

wrestlers
güreşçiler

PLACES AND BUILDINGS

YERLER VE YAPILAR

airport **havalimanı**	*beach* **plaj**
aquarium **akvaryum**	*bridge* **köprü**
bank **banka**	*bungalow* **kır evi**
bay **koy**	*café* **kafeterye**
bazar **pazar**	*canal* **kanal**

castle
kale

circus
sirk

cathedral
katedral

clinic
klinik

cave
mağara

coast
sahil

church
kilise

college
kolej

cinema
sinema

cottage
kulübe

court **mahkeme**	*farm* **çiftlik**
den **in**	*apartment* **apartman**
desert **çöl**	*forest* **orman**
dome **kubbe**	*fort* **kale**
factory **fabrika**	*gallery* **galeri**

petrol station **benzin istasyonu**	*hospital* **hastane**
garden **bahçe**	*hostel* **han**
glacier **buzul**	*hotel* **otel**
gulf **körfez**	*house* **ev**
hills **tepeler**	*hut* **kulübe**

inn
han

library
kütüphane

island
ada

light house
fener

laboratory
laboratuvar

market
çarşı

lake
göl

monument
anıt

lane
yol

mosque
cami

mountain
dağ

orchard
meyva bahçesi

museum
müze

palace
saray

observatory
gözlemevi

park
park

ocean
okyanus

pavement
kaldırım

office
büro

pillars
sütunlar

play ground **oyun alanı**	*prison* **cezaevi**
pond **gölcük**	*restaurant* **lokanta**
pool **havuz**	*river* **ırmak**
port **liman**	*road* **sokak**
post-office **postane**	*school* **okul**

workshop
atölye

station
istasyon

shop
dükkan

street
cadde

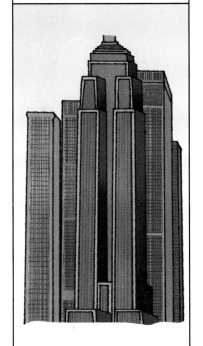

skyscrapers
gökdelenler

subway
altgeçit

super-
market
süpermarket

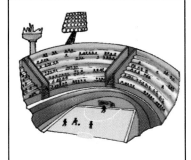

stadium
stadyum

swimming
pool
yüzme
havuzu

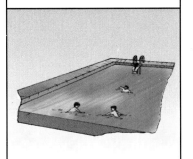

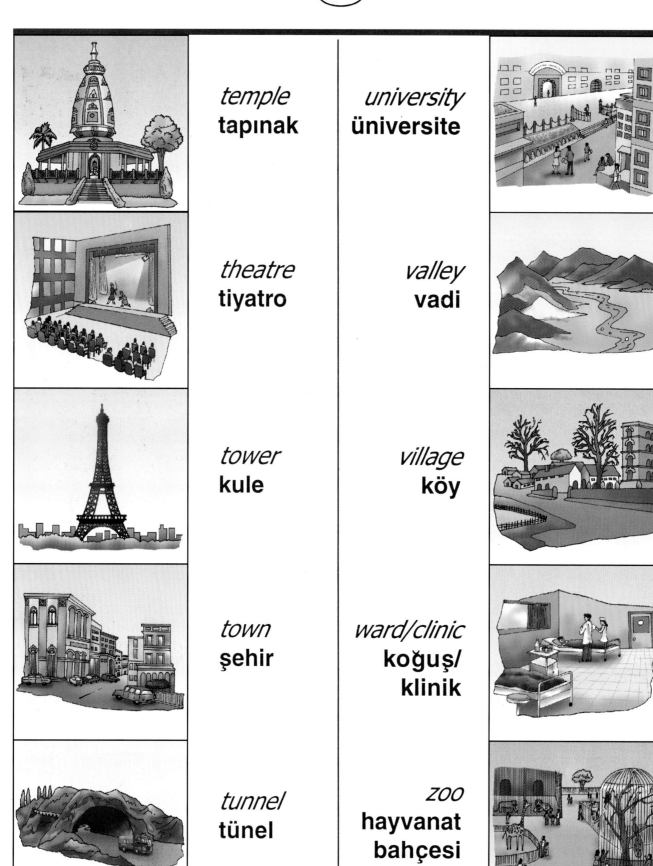

temple **tapınak**	*university* **üniversite**
theatre **tiyatro**	*valley* **vadi**
tower **kule**	*village* **köy**
town **şehir**	*ward/clinic* **koğuş/ klinik**
tunnel **tünel**	*zoo* **hayvanat bahçesi**

PLANTS AND FLOWERS
BİTKİLER VE ÇİÇEKLER

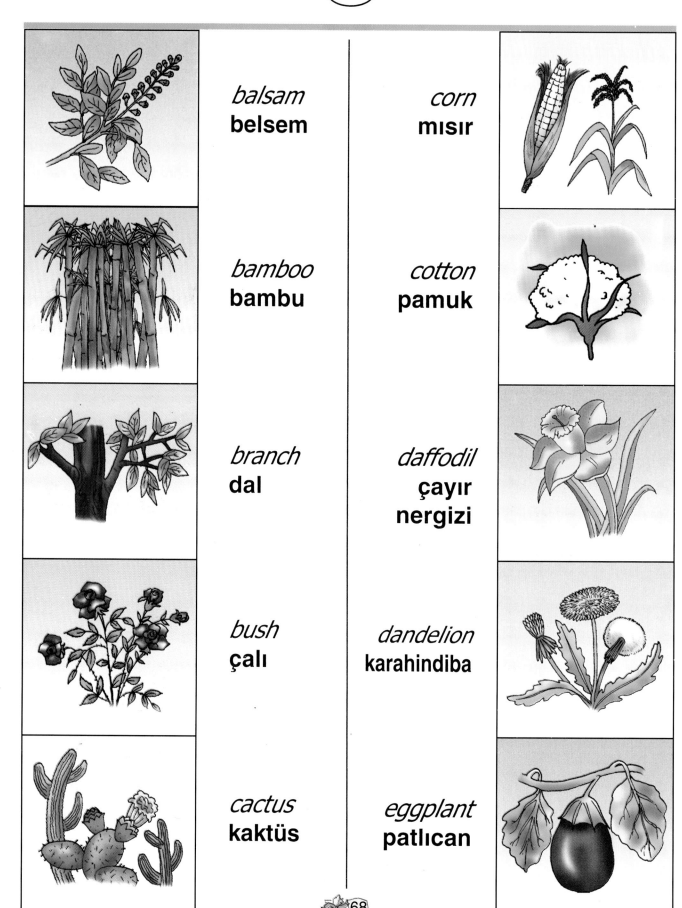

balsam
belsem

bamboo
bambu

branch
dal

bush
çalı

cactus
kaktüs

corn
mısır

cotton
pamuk

daffodil
çayır
nergizi

dandelion
karahindiba

eggplant
patlıcan

elm **karaağaç**	*honey-suckle* **hanımeli**
fir **kozak/ köknar**	*jasmine* **yasemin**
flax **keten**	*lily* **zambak**
grass **çim**	*maize* **mısır**
heliopsis **vanilya çiçeği**	*narcissus* **nergis**

olive **zeytin**	sugarcanes **şeker kamışları**
palm trees **palmiye**	tobacco **tütün**
peas **bezelye**	vanilla **vanilya**
root **kök**	water-lilies **nilüferler**
rose **gül**	zinnias **zinia çiçekleri**

SPORTS, GAMES AND RECREATION
SPOR, OYUNLAR VE EĞLENCE

arrows **oklar**	*billiard* **bilardo**
archery **yay**	*carrom board* **karom**
badminton **badminton**	*chess* **satranç**
ball **top**	*clarinet* **klarnet**
balloons **balonlar**	*cornet* **karnet**

drum
davul

flute
flüt

cricket
kriket

football
futbol

golf
golf

guitar
gitar

hockey
hokey

kite
uçurtma

mandolin
mandolin

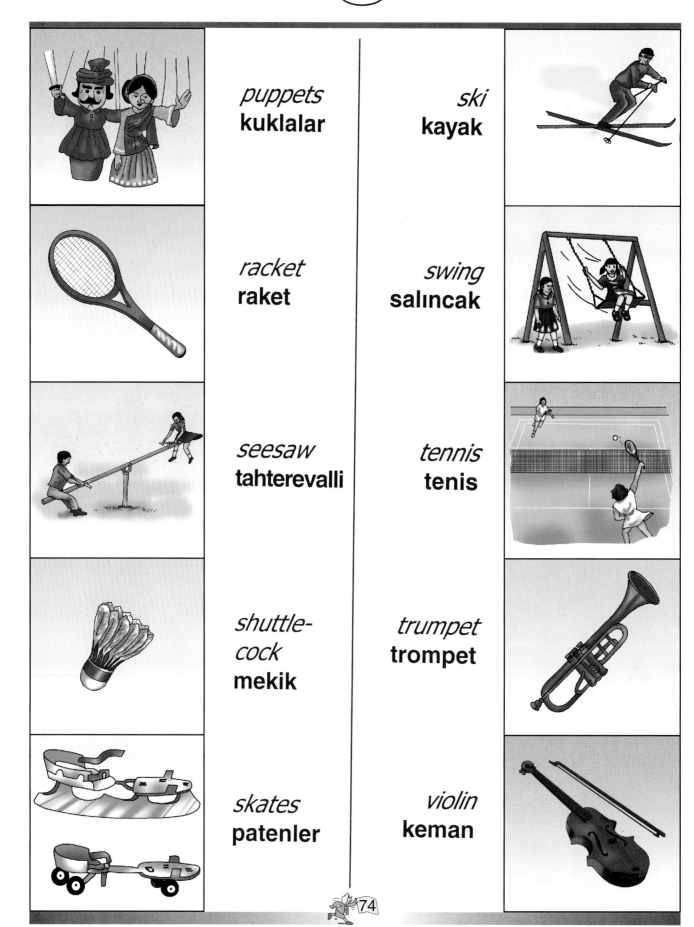

puppets **kuklalar**	*ski* **kayak**
racket **raket**	*swing* **salıncak**
seesaw **tahterevalli**	*tennis* **tenis**
shuttle-cock **mekik**	*trumpet* **trompet**
skates **patenler**	*violin* **keman**

TRANSPORT AND COMMUNICATION
ULAŞIM VE İLETİŞİM

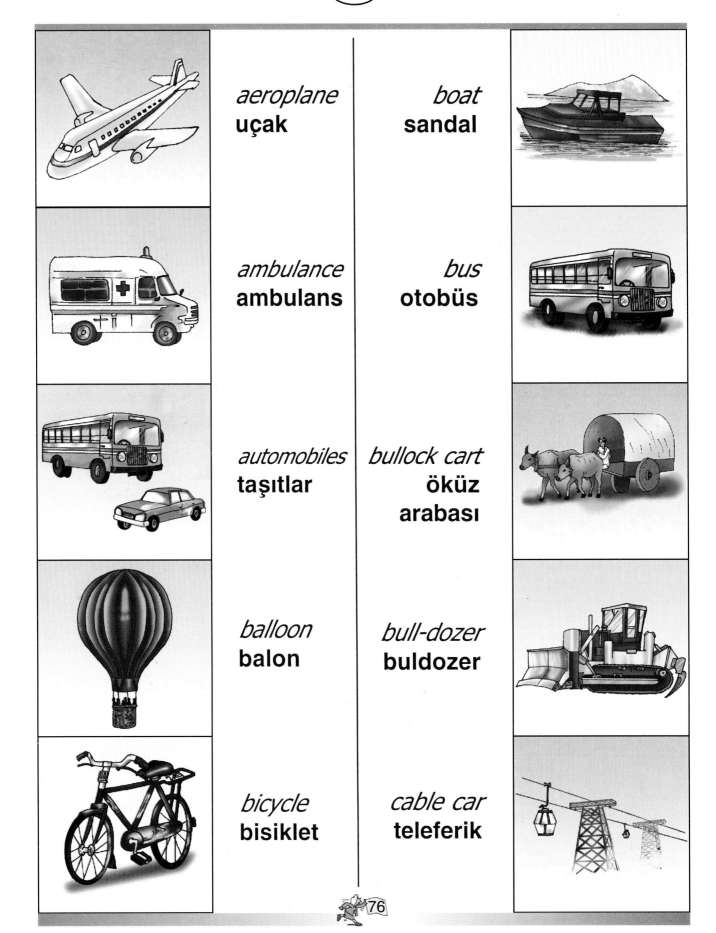

aeroplane **uçak**	*boat* **sandal**
ambulance **ambulans**	*bus* **otobüs**
automobiles **taşıtlar**	*bullock cart* **öküz arabası**
balloon **balon**	*bull-dozer* **buldozer**
bicycle **bisiklet**	*cable car* **teleferik**

car **otomobil**	*crane* **vinç**
caravan **karavan**	*double decker bus* iki katlı otobüs (şehiriçi)
cart **el arabası**	*engine (railway)* **lokomotif**
chariot **savaş arabası**	*fax* **fax makinesi**
coach **otobüs** (şehirlerarası)	*fire-engine* **itfaiye**

generator **jeneratör**	*motorcycle* **motorsiklet**
helicopter **helikopter**	*parachute* **paraşüt**
hover-craft **hoverkraft**	*petrol pumps* **benzin pompaları**
jeep **jip**	*post-card* **kartpostal**
letter **mektup**	*radio* **radyo**

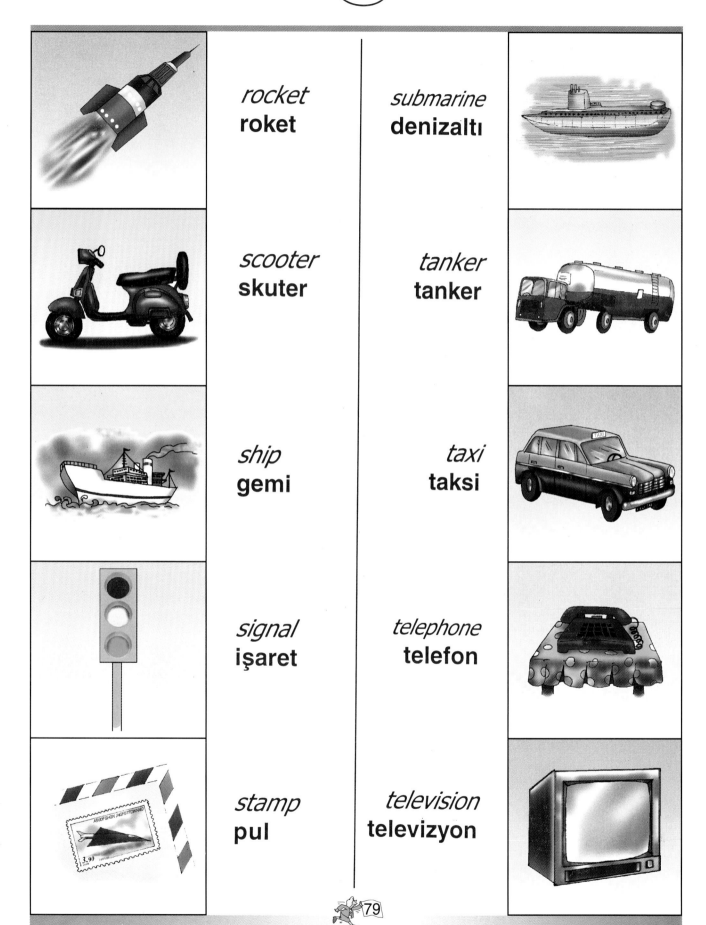

rocket **roket**	*submarine* **denizaltı**
scooter **skuter**	*tanker* **tanker**
ship **gemi**	*taxi* **taksi**
signal **işaret**	*telephone* **telefon**
stamp **pul**	*television* **televizyon**

typewriter
daktilo

tram-car
tramvay

tractor
traktör

van
kamyonet

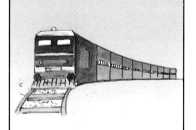

train
tren

vehicles
taşıtlar

tricycle
üç tekerlekli
bisiklet

wheel
tekerlek

tri-shaw
bisiklet
taksisi

yacht
yat

UNIVERSE AND WEATHER

EVREN VE HAVA

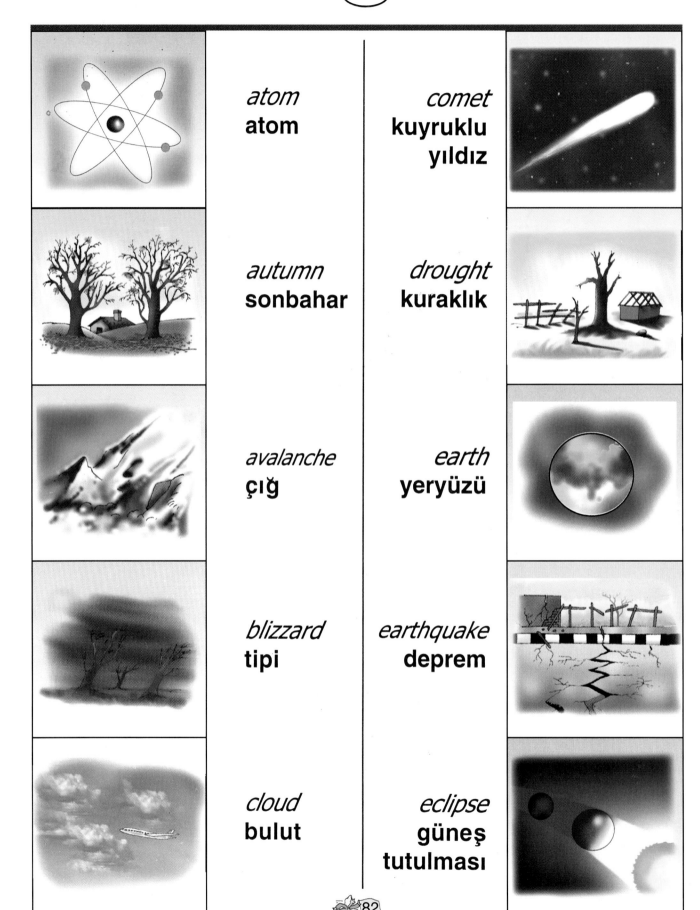

atom **atom**	*comet* **kuyruklu yıldız**
autumn **sonbahar**	*drought* **kuraklık**
avalanche **çığ**	*earth* **yeryüzü**
blizzard **tipi**	*earthquake* **deprem**
cloud **bulut**	*eclipse* **güneş tutulması**

flood **tufan**	*orbit* **yörünge**	
fog **sis**	*rain* **yağmur**	
globe **dünya**	*satellite* **uydu**	
lightning **şimşek**	*sky* **gökyüzü**	
map **harita**	*snow* **kar**	

OTHER USEFUL WORDS
DİĞER YARARLI SÖZCÜKLER

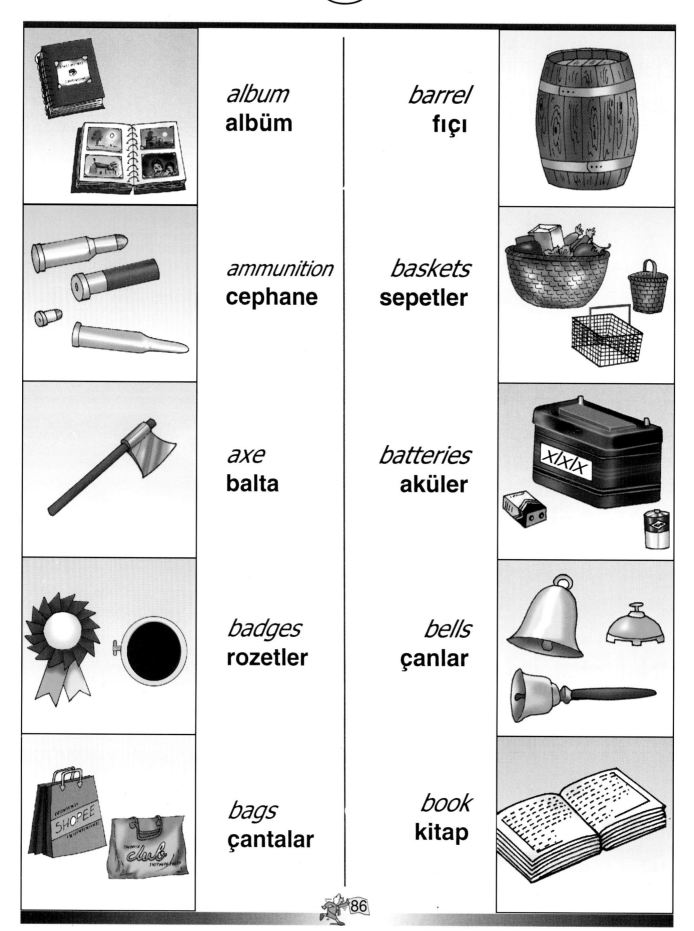

album **albüm**	*barrel* **fıçı**
ammunition **cephane**	*baskets* **sepetler**
axe **balta**	*batteries* **aküler**
badges **rozetler**	*bells* **çanlar**
bags **çantalar**	*book* **kitap**

bottles **şişeler**	*buttons* **düğmeler**
box **kutu**	*cable* **kablo**
bricks **tuğlalar**	*cage* **kafes**
brushes **fırçalar**	*camera* **fotoğraf makinesi**
belt **kemer**	*candle* **mum**

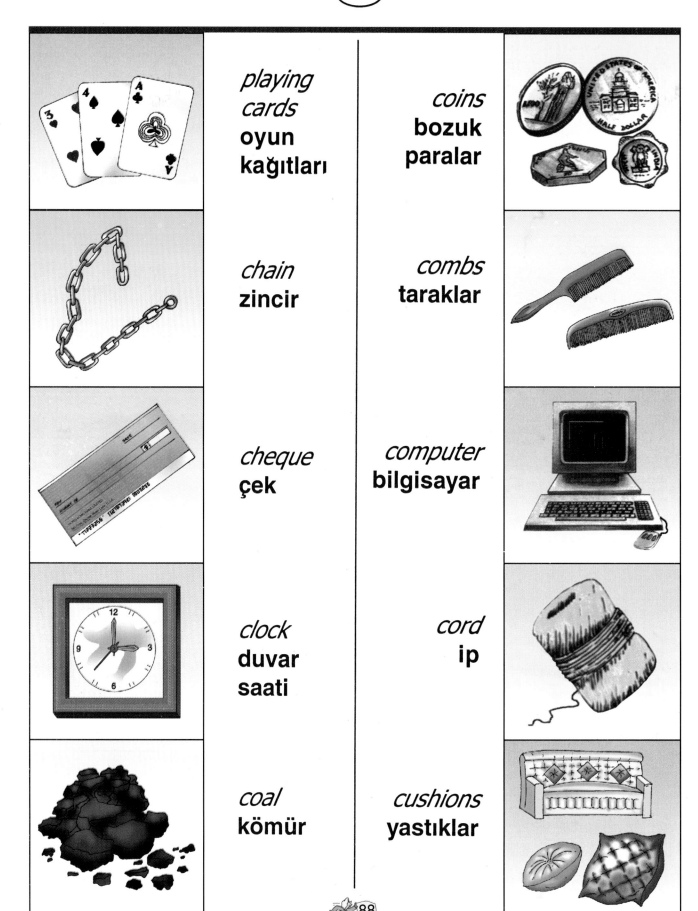

playing cards **oyun kağıtları**	*coins* **bozuk paralar**
chain **zincir**	*combs* **taraklar**
cheque **çek**	*computer* **bilgisayar**
clock **duvar saati**	*cord* **ip**
coal **kömür**	*cushions* **yastıklar**

cylinder **silindir**	*drugs* **ilaçlar**
dagger **hançer**	*dustbin* **çöp kutusu**
desk **yazı masası**	*envelopes* **zarflar**
dish **tabak**	*eraser* **silgi**
drawer **çekmece**	*fans* **vantilatörler**

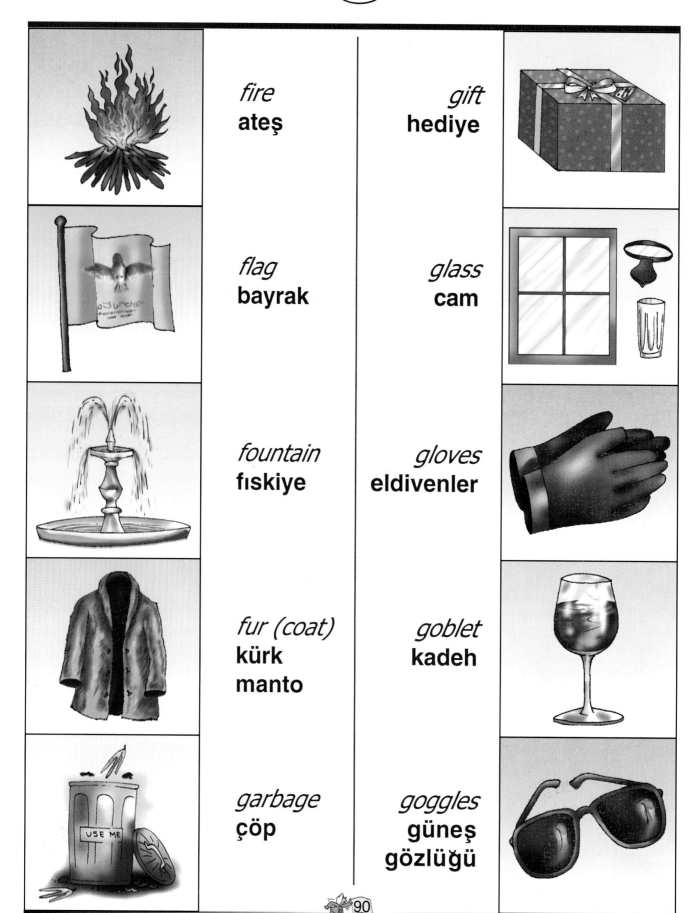

fire **ateş**	*gift* **hediye**
flag **bayrak**	*glass* **cam**
fountain **fıskiye**	*gloves* **eldivenler**
fur (coat) **kürk** **manto**	*goblet* **kadeh**
garbage **çöp**	*goggles* **güneş gözlüğü**

gum/glue **zamk**	*hats* **şapkalar**
guns **silahlar**	*helmet* **miğfer**
hammer **çekiç**	*ink* **mürekkep**
handker-chief **mendil**	*ivory* **fildişi**
handles **kulplar/ saplar**	*jar* **kavanoz**

jug **su kabı**	*lace* **ayakkabı bağı**
kettle **su ısıtıcısı**	*ladder* **merdiven**
keys **anahtarlar**	*leather* **deri**
knives **bıçaklar**	*lens* **büyüteç**
labels **etiketler**	*letters* **mektuplar**

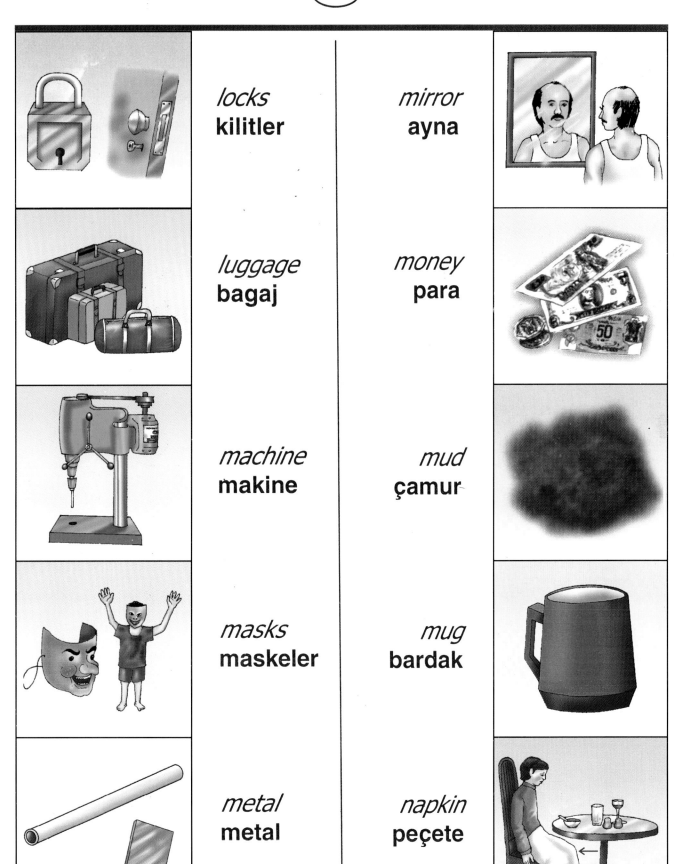

locks **kilitler**	*mirror* **ayna**
luggage **bagaj**	*money* **para**
machine **makine**	*mud* **çamur**
masks **maskeler**	*mug* **bardak**
metal **metal**	*napkin* **peçete**

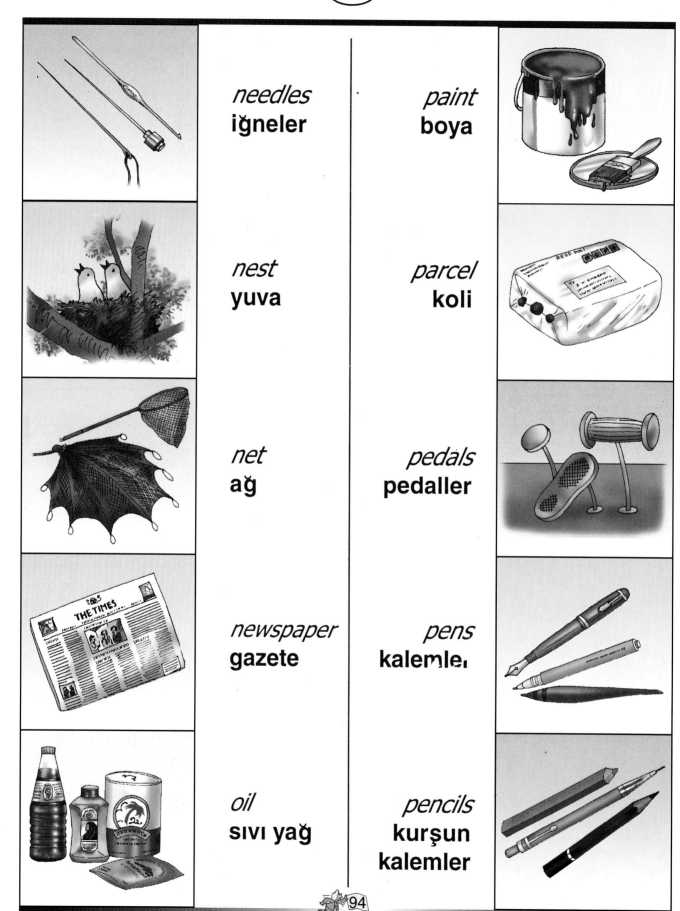

needles	paint
iğneler	boya
nest	parcel
yuva	koli
net	pedals
ağ	pedaller
newspaper	pens
gazete	kalemler
oil	pencils
sıvı yağ	kurşun kalemler

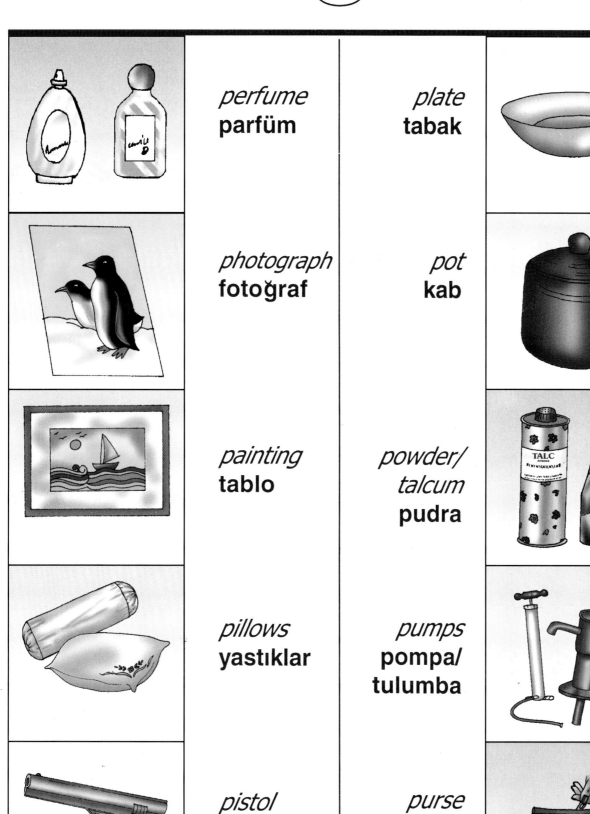

perfume **parfüm**	*plate* **tabak**
photograph **fotoğraf**	*pot* **kab**
painting **tablo**	*powder/* *talcum* **pudra**
pillows **yastıklar**	*pumps* **pompa/** **tulumba**
pistol **tabanca**	*purse* **para** **çantası**

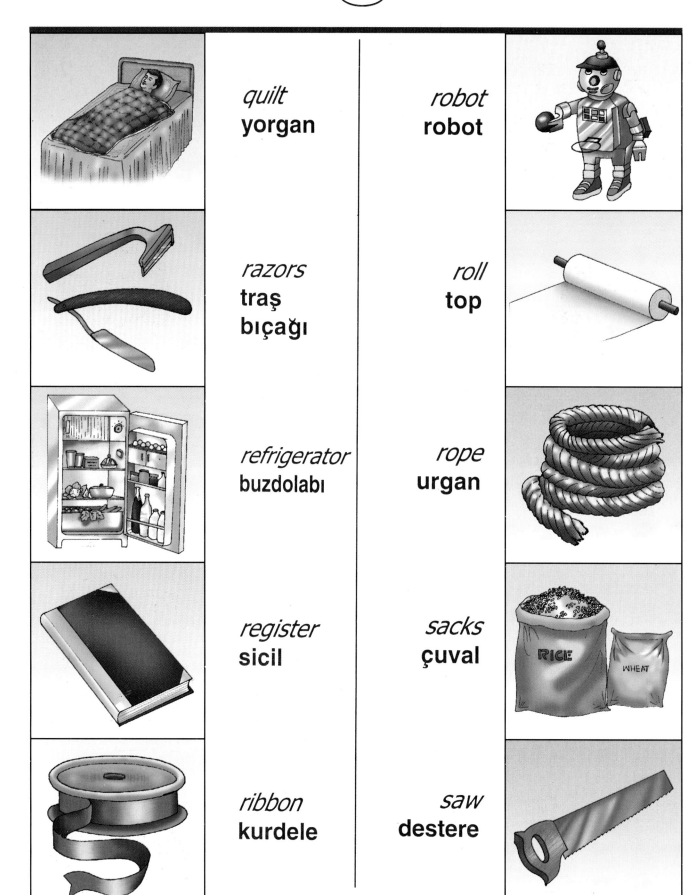

quilt **yorgan**	*robot* **robot**
razors **traş bıçağı**	*roll* **top**
refrigerator **buzdolabı**	*rope* **urgan**
register **sicil**	*sacks* **çuval**
ribbon **kurdele**	*saw* **destere**

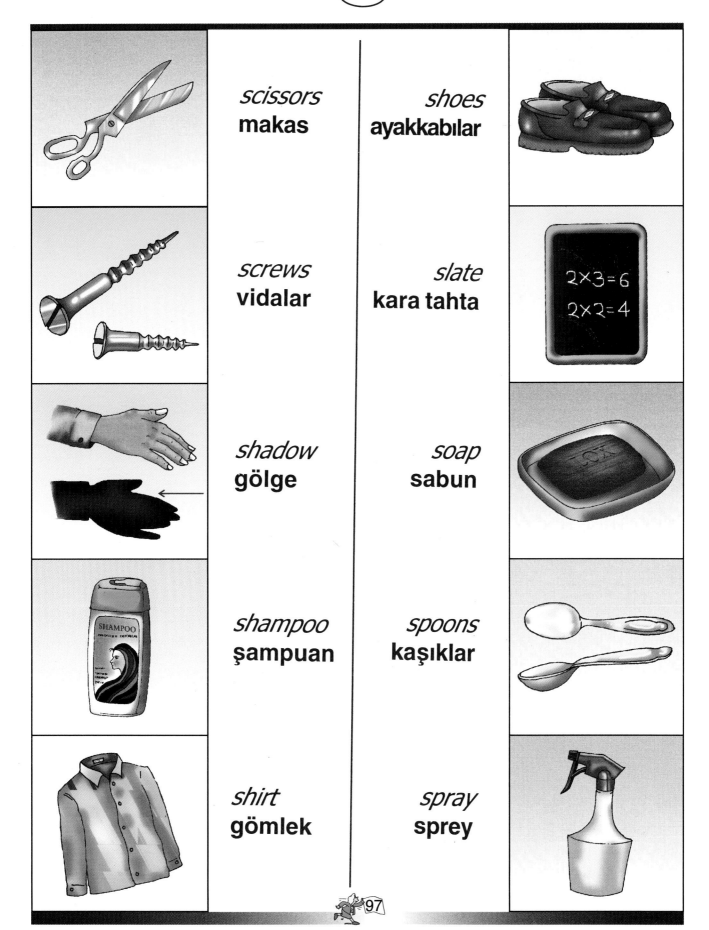

	scissors **makas**	*shoes* **ayakkabılar**
	screws **vidalar**	*slate* **kara tahta**
	shadow **gölge**	*soap* **sabun**
	shampoo **şampuan**	*spoons* **kaşıklar**
	shirt **gömlek**	*spray* **sprey**

$2 \times 3 = 6$

$2 \times 2 = 4$

statue **heykel**	*tickets* **biletler**
stethoscope **dinleme aleti**	*timber* **kereste**
socks **çoraplar**	*tins* **tenekeler**
teapot **çaydanlık**	*tools* **aletler**
thread **iplik**	*towels* **havlular**

mouse-trap **kapan**	*typewriter* **daktilo**
tray **tepsi**	*umbrella* **şemsiye**
treasure **hazine**	*utensils* **mutfak takımı**
tubes **tüpler**	*vaseline* **vazelin**
turban **sarık**	*vault* **depo**

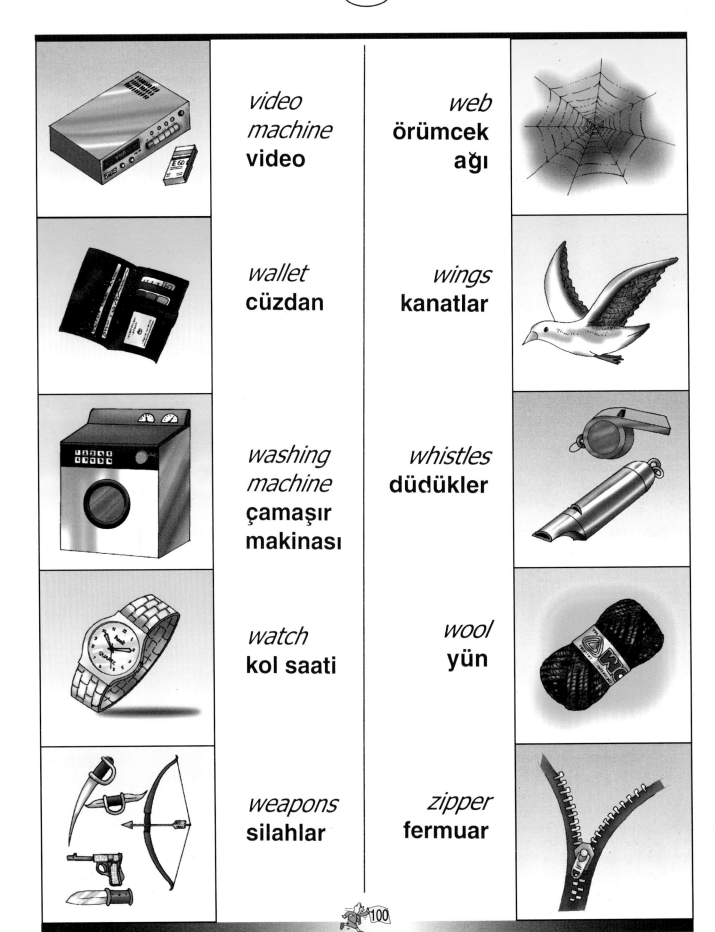

video machine **video**	*web* **örümcek ağı**
wallet **cüzdan**	*wings* **kanatlar**
washing machine **çamaşır makinası**	*whistles* **düdükler**
watch **kol saati**	*wool* **yün**
weapons **silahlar**	*zipper* **fermuar**